I0471111

Erin Ontario in Photos, Saving Our History One Photo at a Time

Photography
by Barbara Raué
2012

Series Name:
Cruising Ontario

Book 22: Erin

Cover photo: #213 – a house from A.D. 1891 with paired cornice brackets, dichromatic brickwork, and iron cresting above the bay window

Series Name: Cruising Ontario

Book 1: London
Book 2: Dundas
Book 3: Hamilton
Book 4: Oakville
Book 5: Chesley
Book 6: Stoney Creek
Book 7: Waterdown
Book 8: Owen Sound
Book 9: Mount Forest
Book 10: Dundalk
Book 11: Burford and Area
Book 12: Waterford and Area
Book 13: Drumbo and Area
Book 14: Sheffield and Area
Book 15: Tavistock and Area
Book 16: Ancaster and Mount Hope
Book 17: Innerkip
Book 18: Brantford
Book 19: Burlington
Book 20: Guelph and Area
Book 21: Ayr
Book 22: Erin

Other Books by Barbara Raue

Coins of Gold

Arrows, Indians and Love

The Life and Times of Barbara
Volume 1: Inventions That Have Enhanced My Life
Volume 2: Entertainment That I Have Enjoyed
Volume 3: East Coast Trips
Volume 4: Olympics
Volume 5: Wonders of the World
Volume 6: Caribbean Cruises
Volume 7: Animals
Volume 8: Storms

Erin

A small community formed here at the headwaters of the Credit and Grand Rivers following the erection of mills on the Credit River in 1828-29. The mills were later rebuilt by Daniel McMillan (in our McMillan family line). In 1839 Erin post office was formed at "McMillan's Mills." In 1851, with a population of 300, the settlement contained several prosperous industries including a distillery, a tannery, and carding, oatmeal and grist-mills. Agricultural prosperity and abundant water power stimulated the community's growth as an important regional centre for milling and the manufacture of wood products. In 1879 a branch of the Credit Valley Railway was completed through Erin to Toronto.

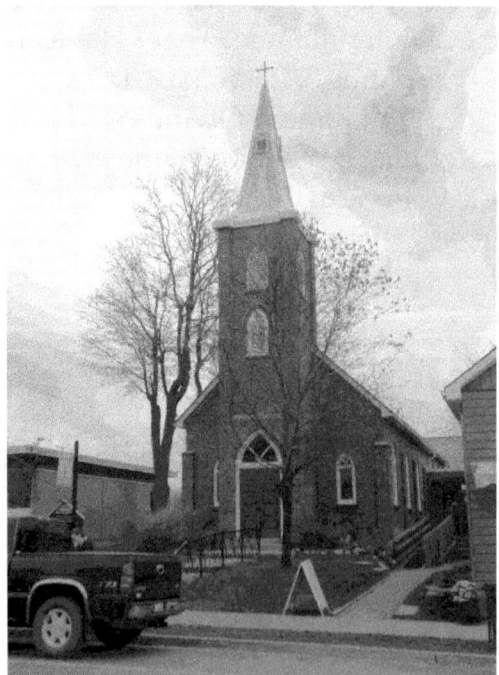

Saints Anglican Church

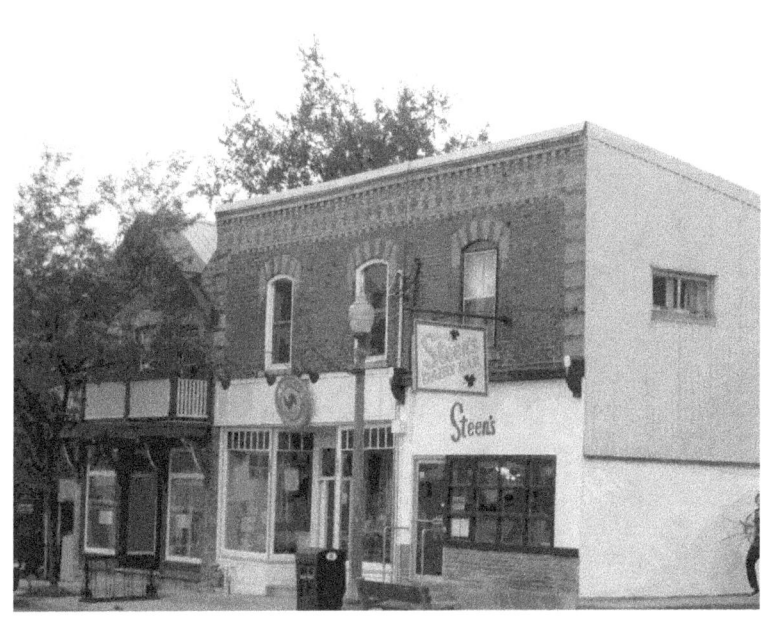

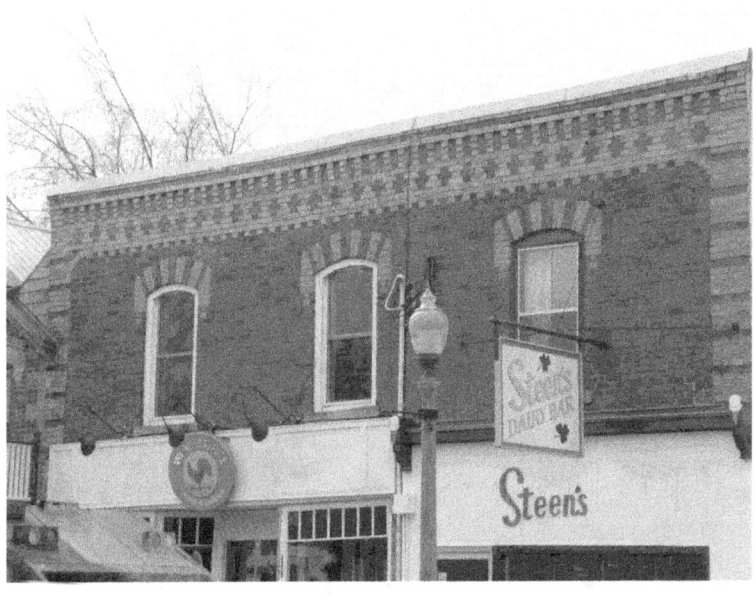

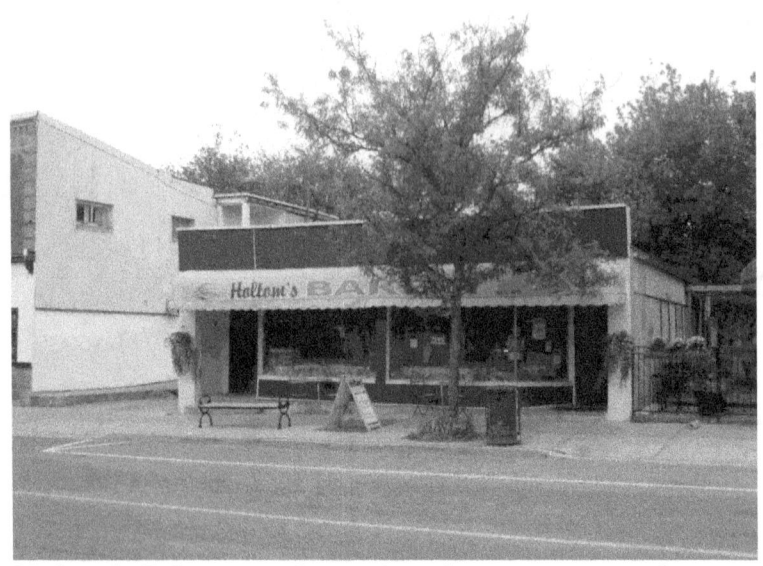

Holton's Bakery – a favourite place to stop on the way through town!

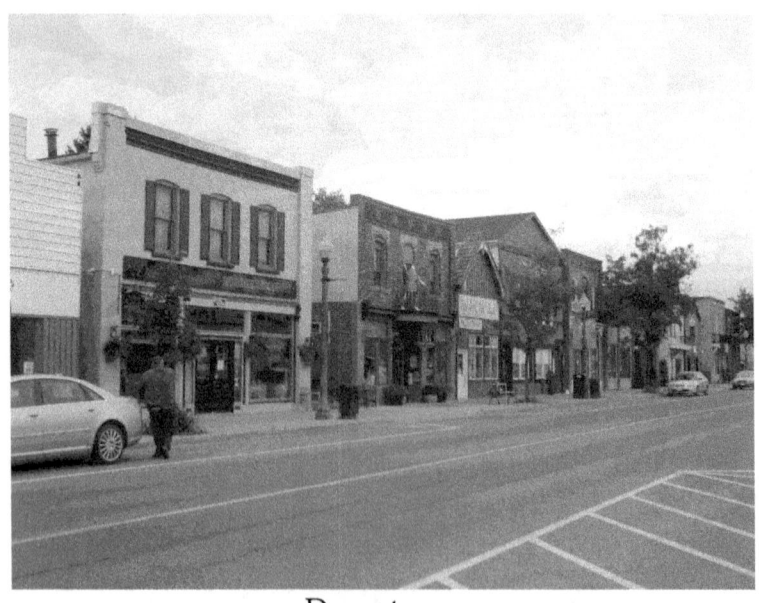

Downtown

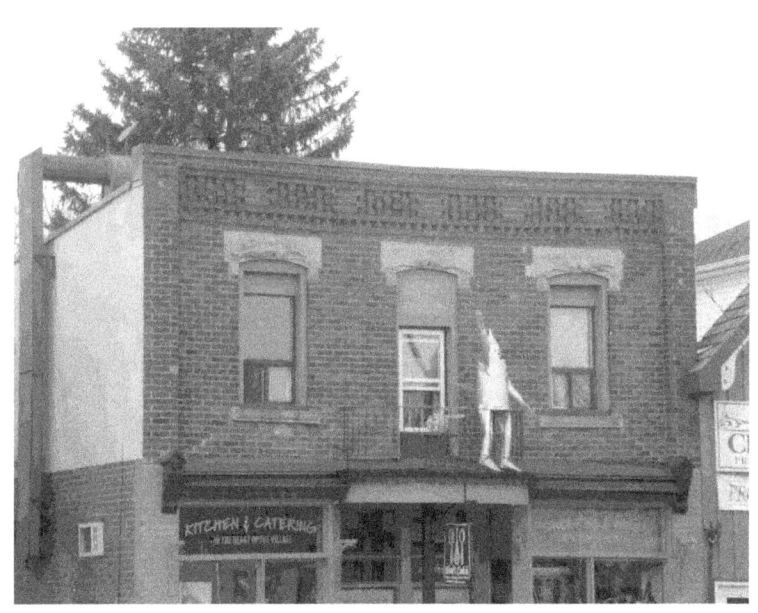

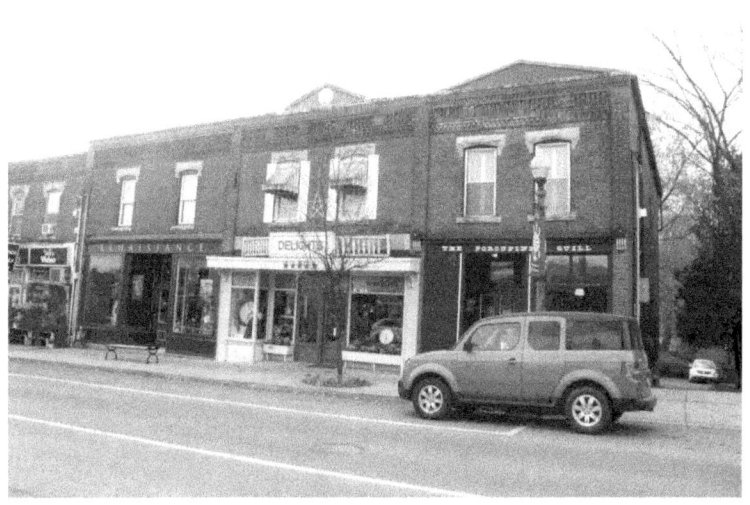

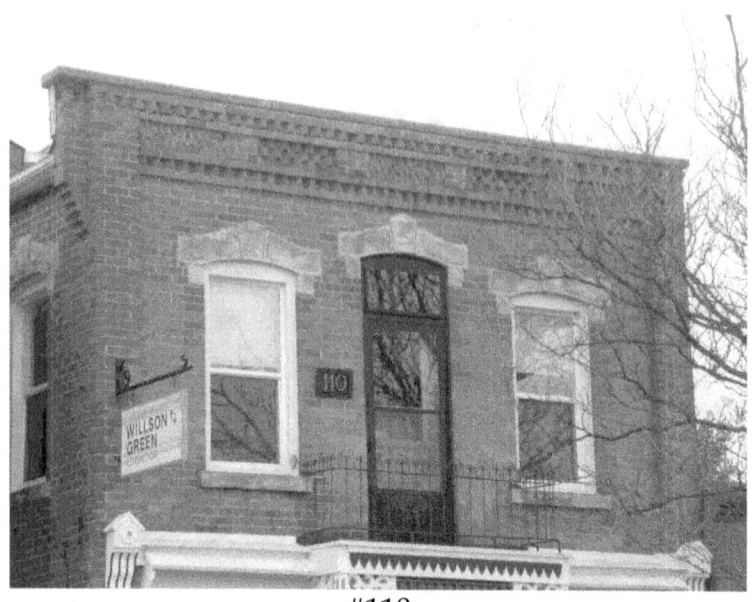

#110

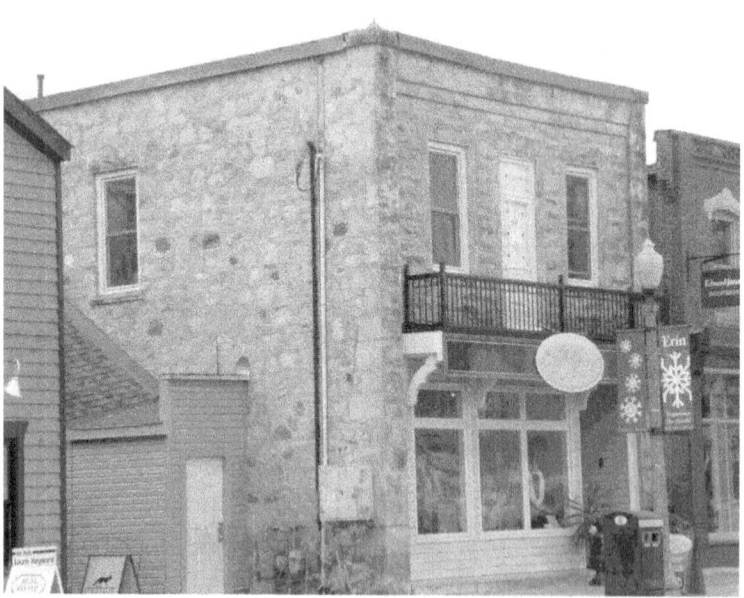

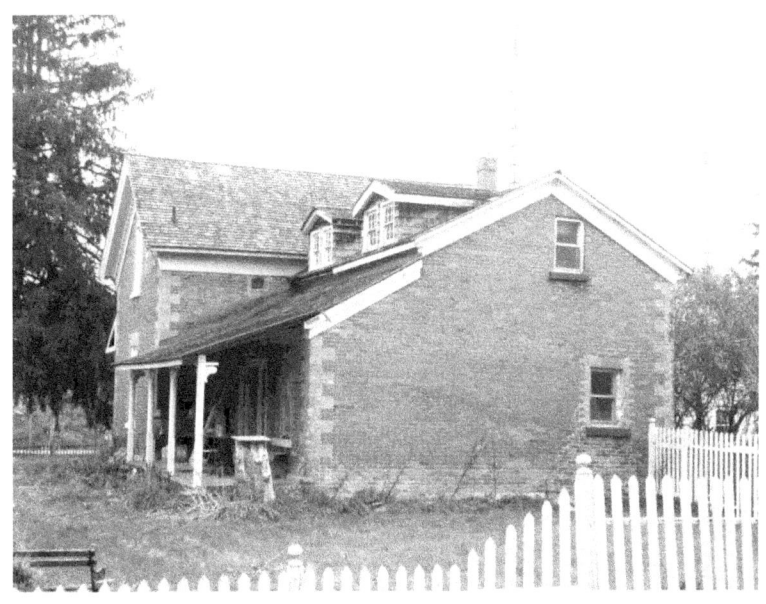

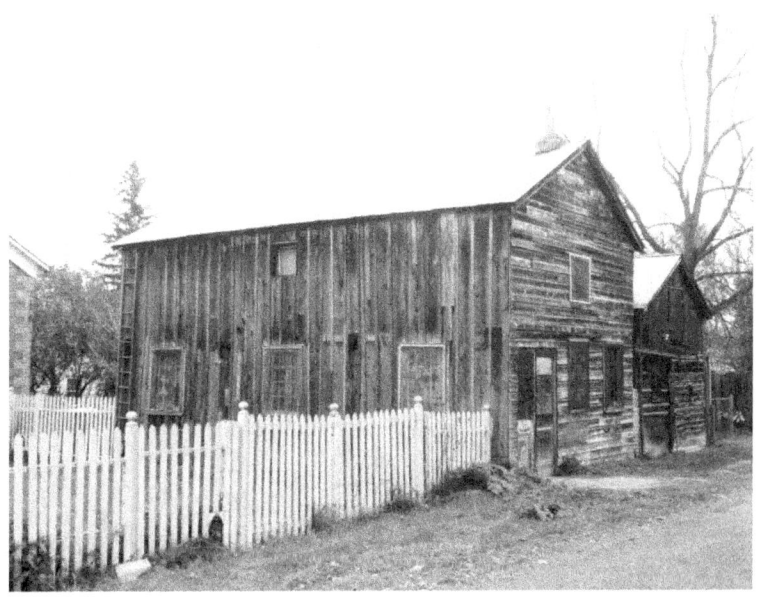

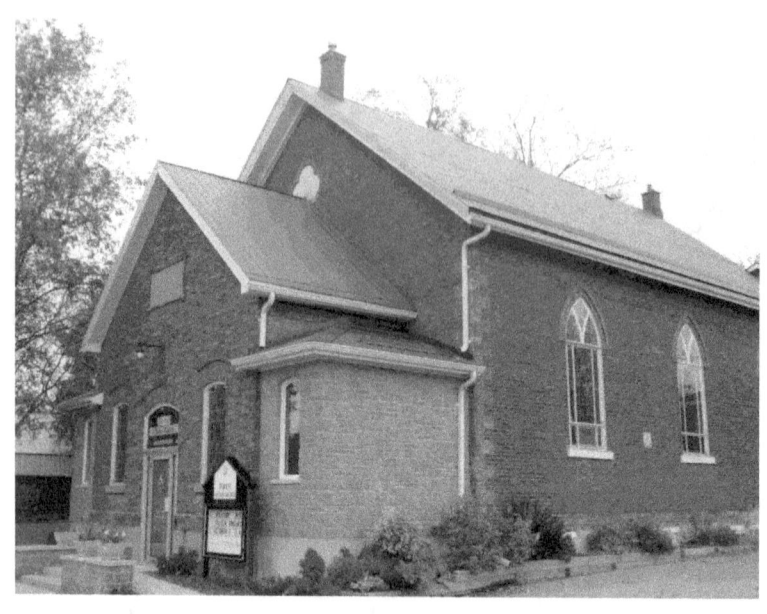

Erin United Church

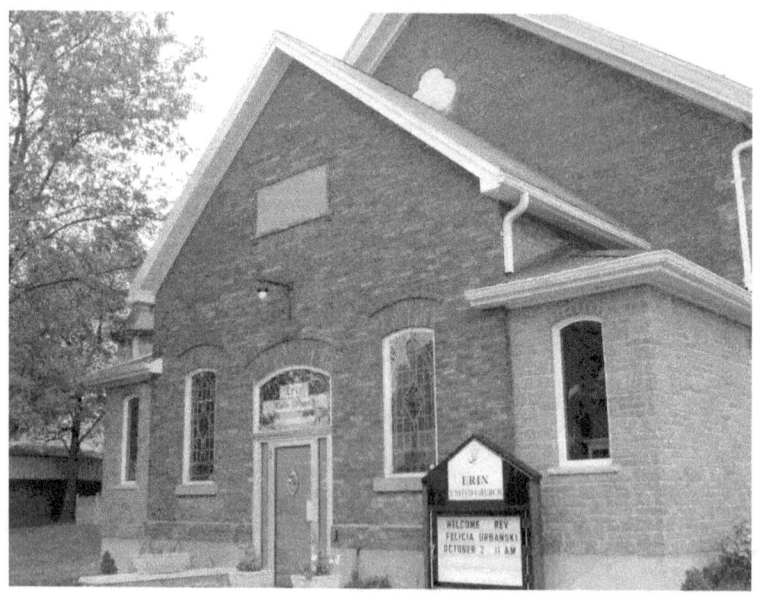

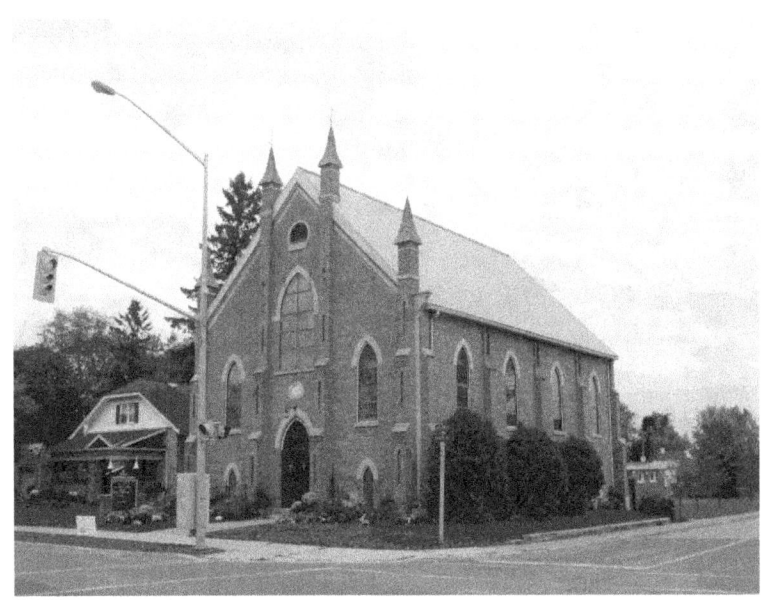

Erin Presbyterian Church

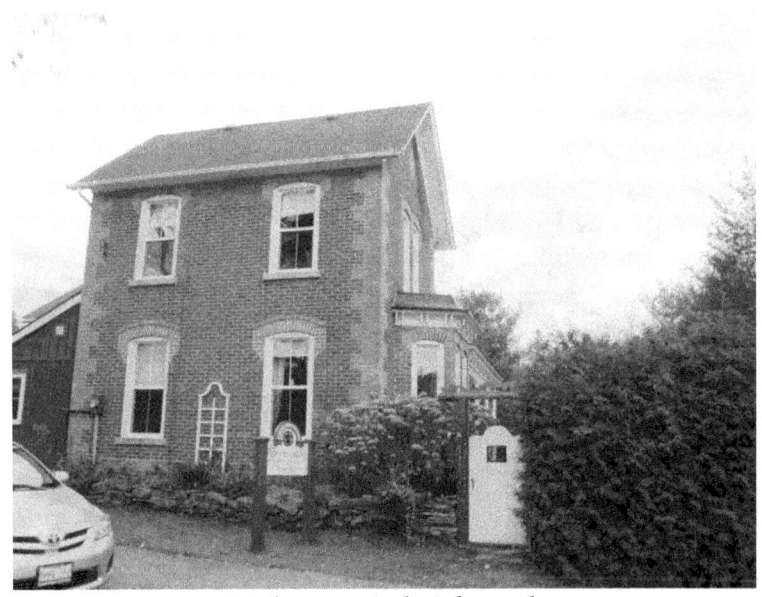

Dichromatic brickwork

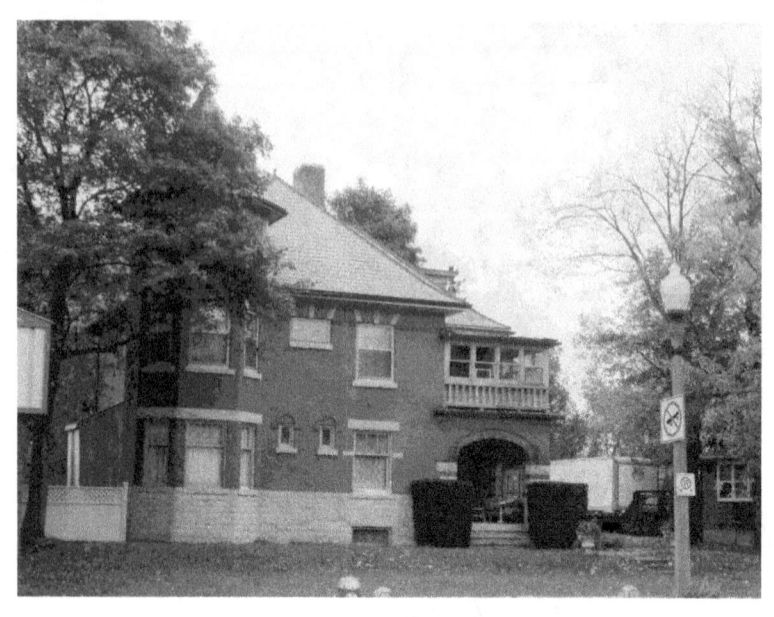

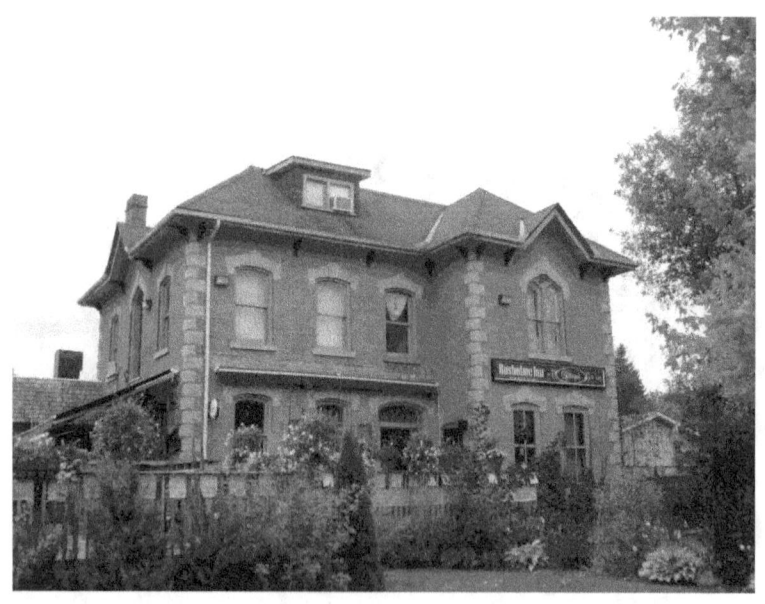

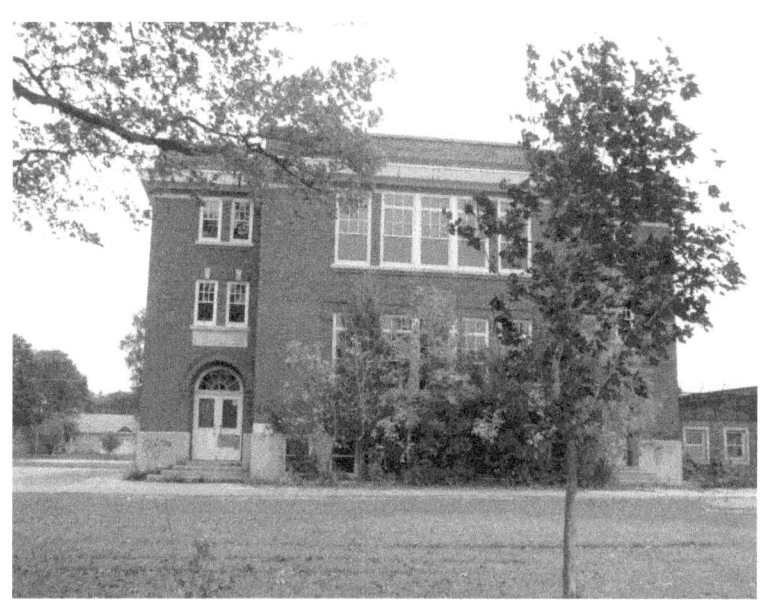

School

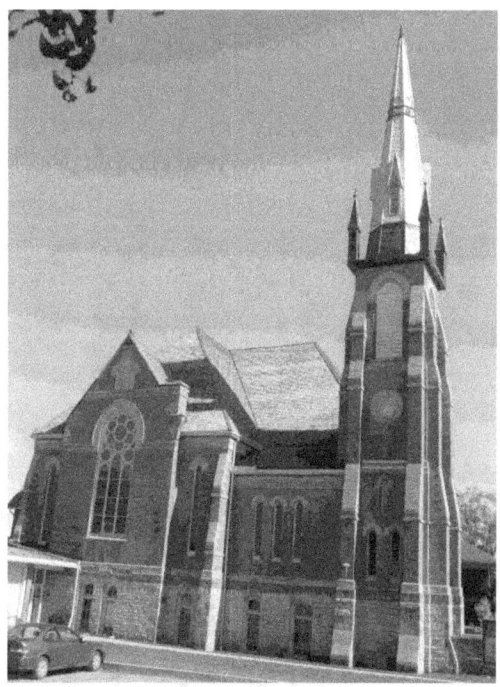

Westminster United Church, 247 Broadway

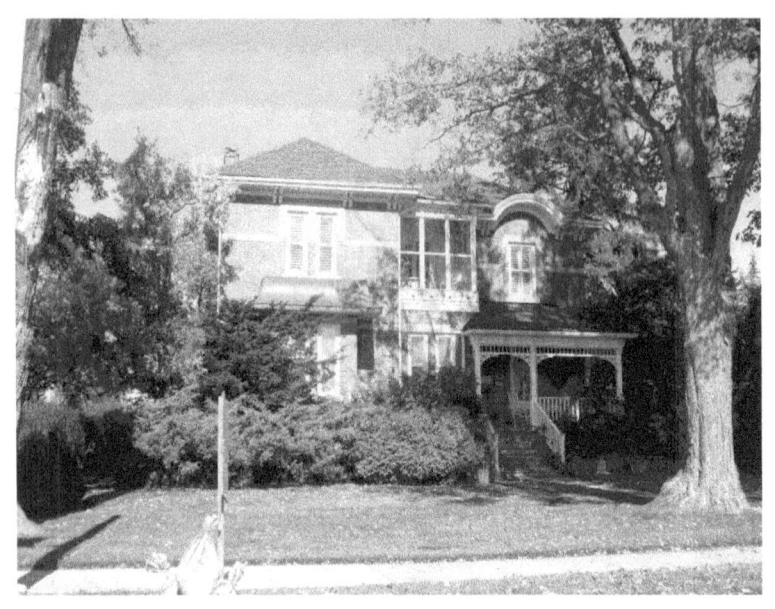

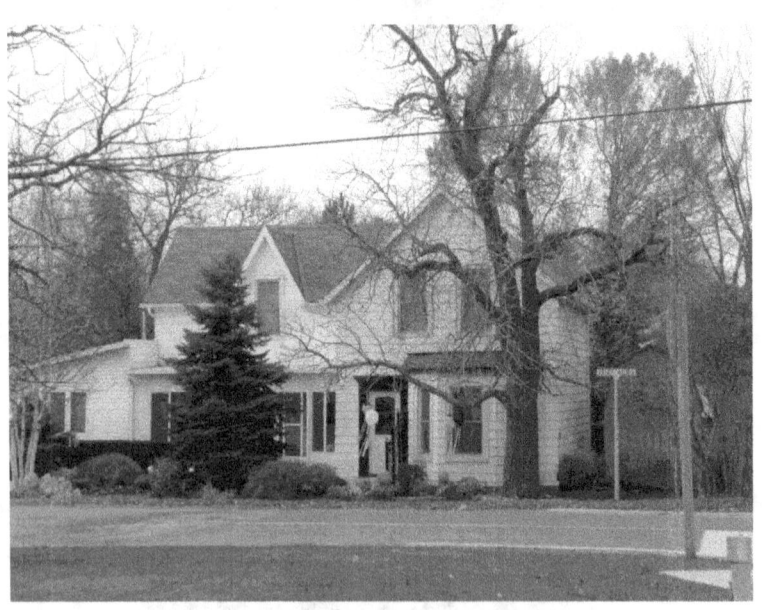

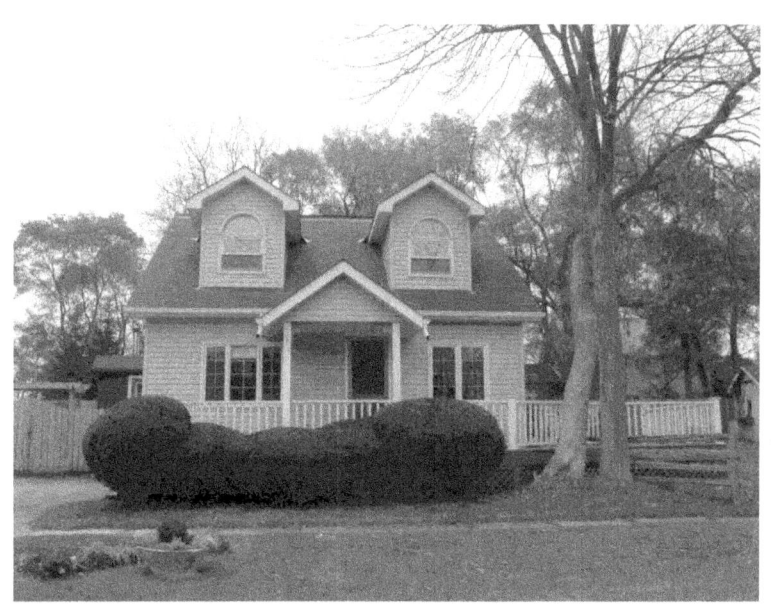

1 Ross

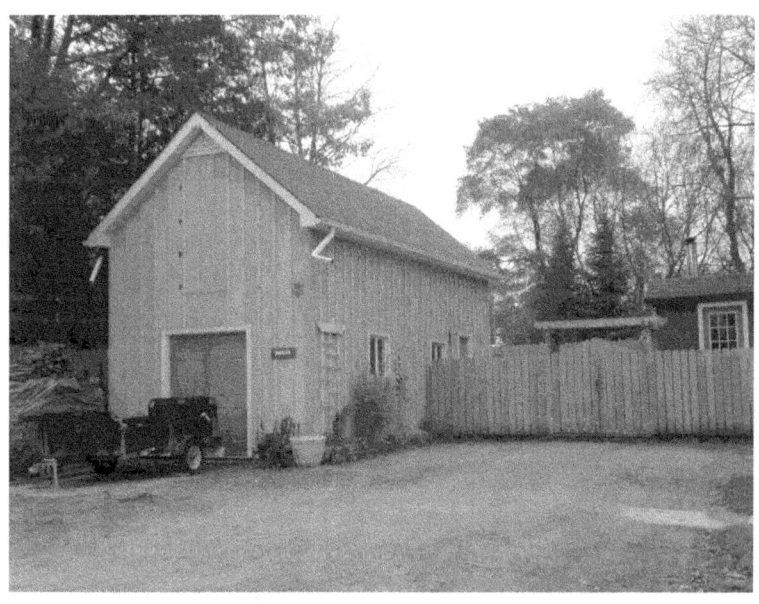

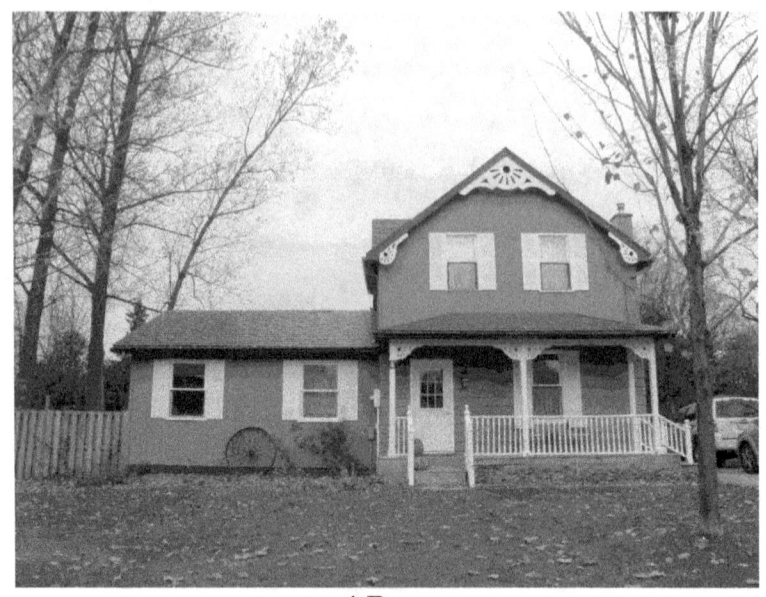

4 Ross

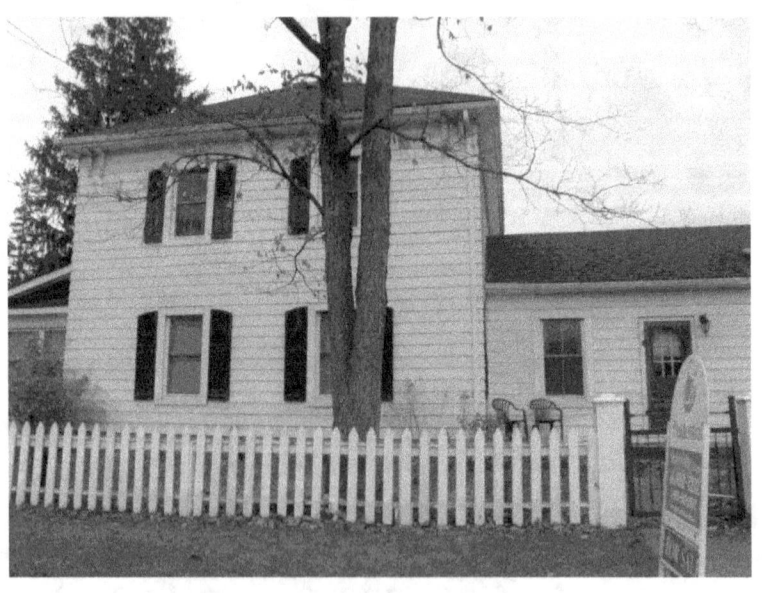

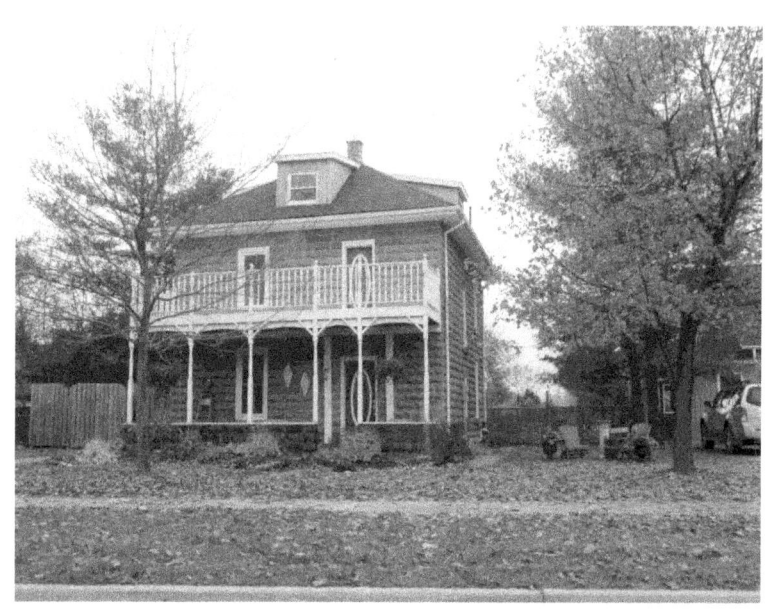

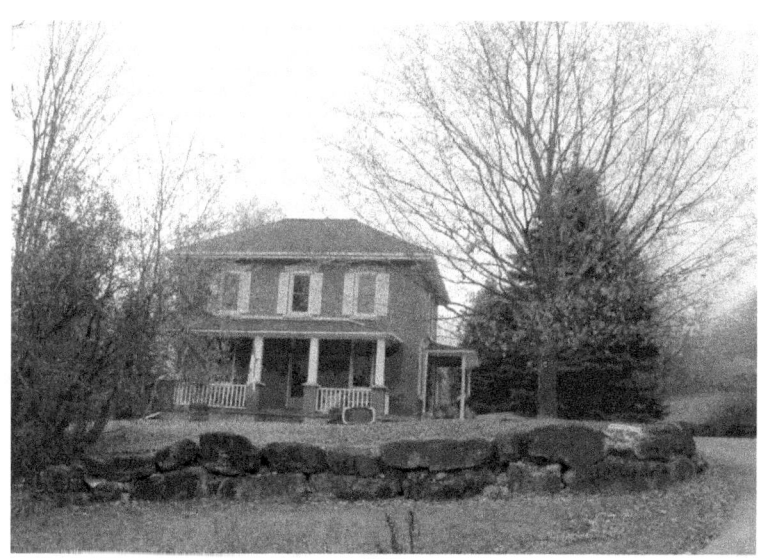

#50

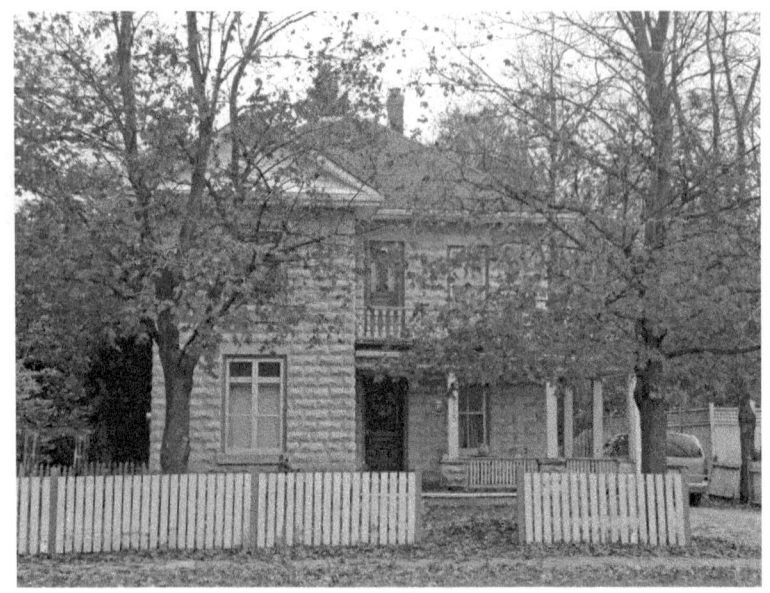

#215

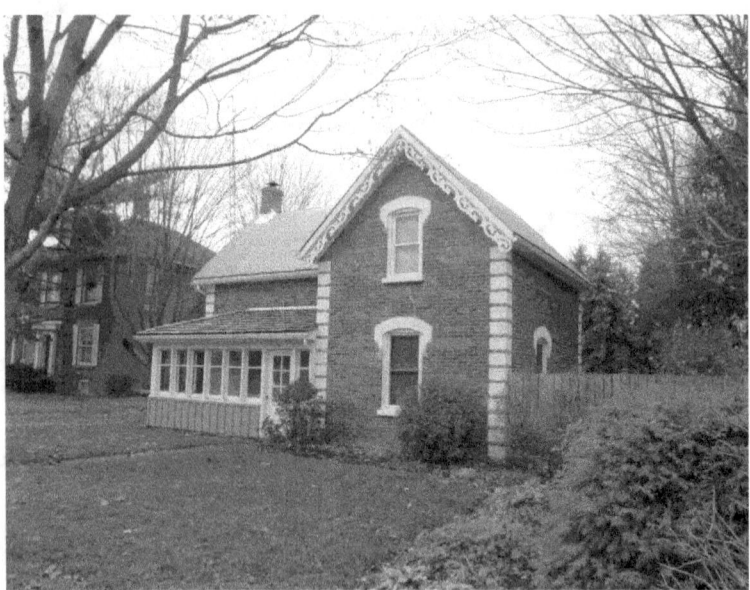

Gingerbread trim, white bricks on corners and above
windows

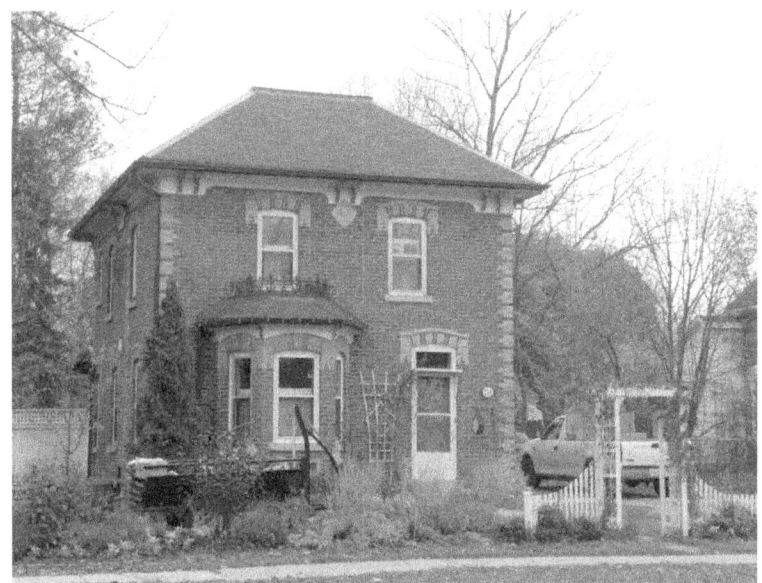

#213 – double cornice brackets, iron cresting above bay
window, dichromatic brickwork - A.D. 1891

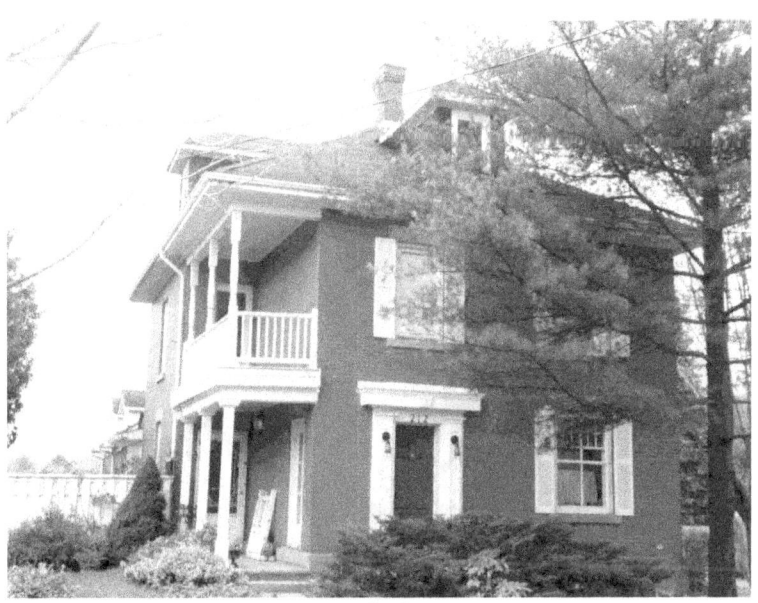

#212

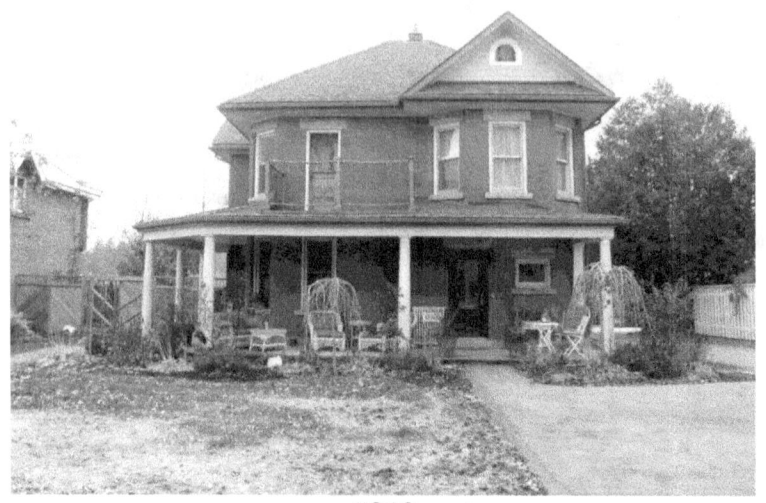

#210

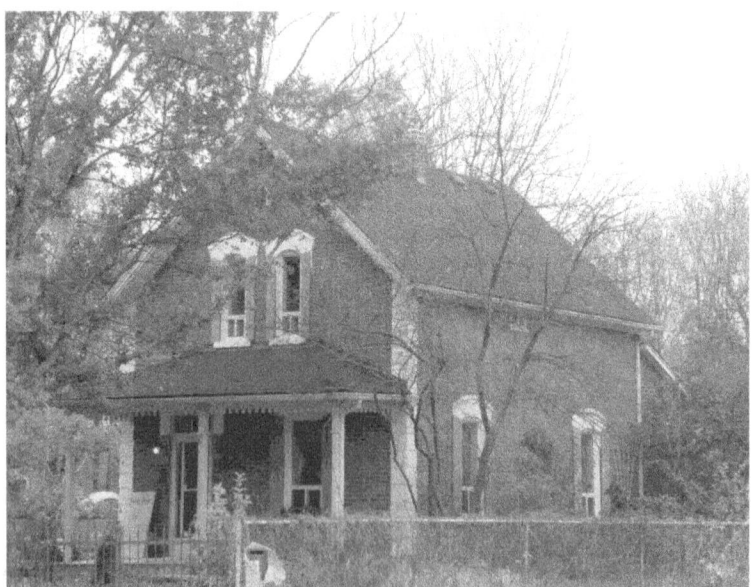

Red brick

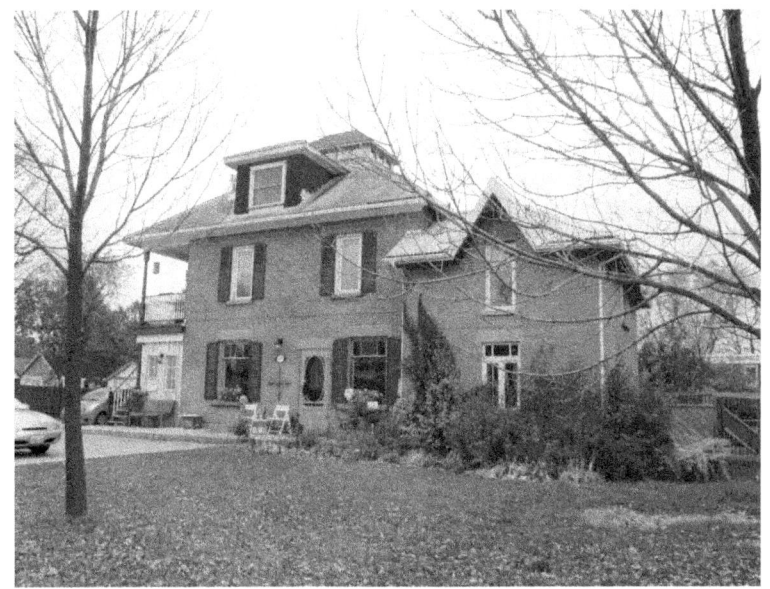

#208

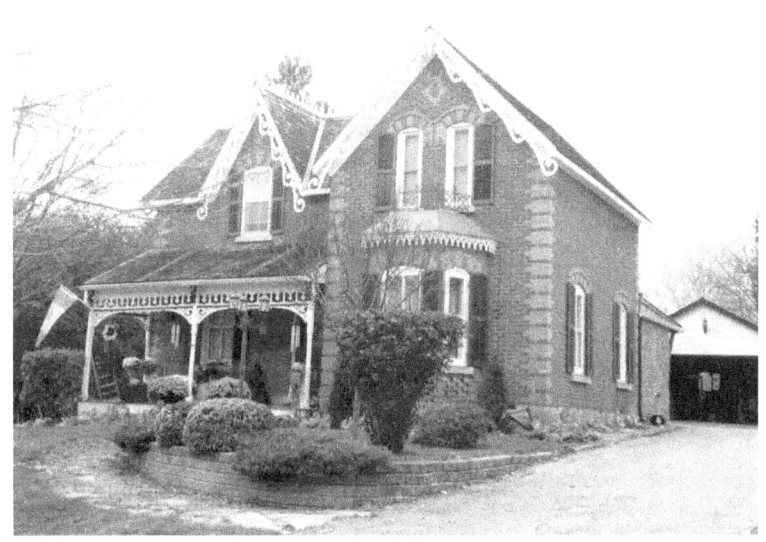

#202

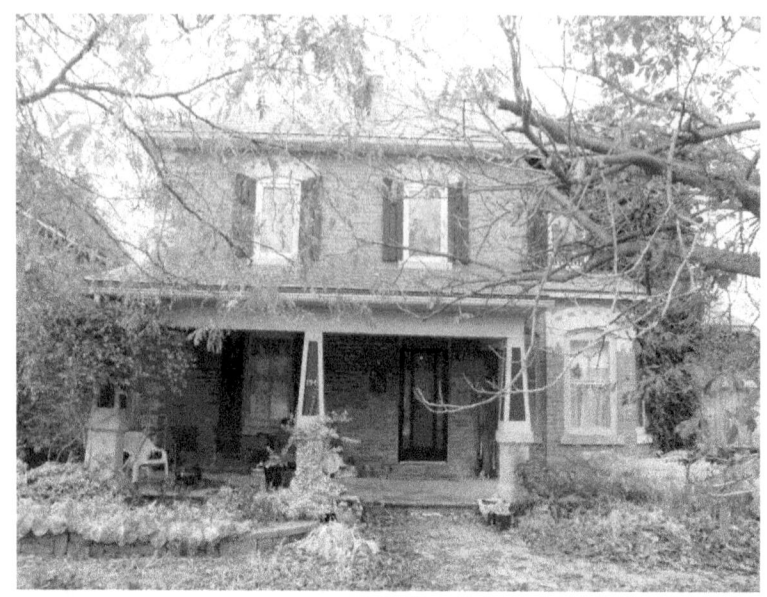

#194

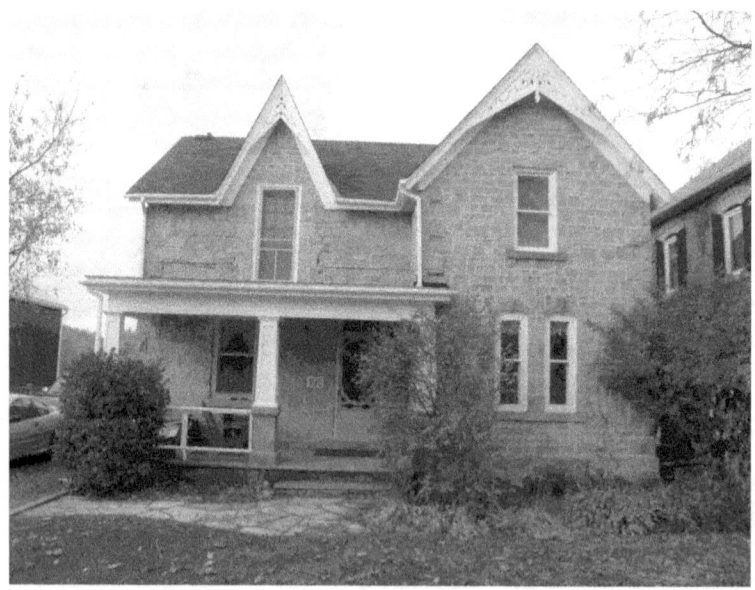

#192 – yellow stone, Gothic style arches with gingerbread trim

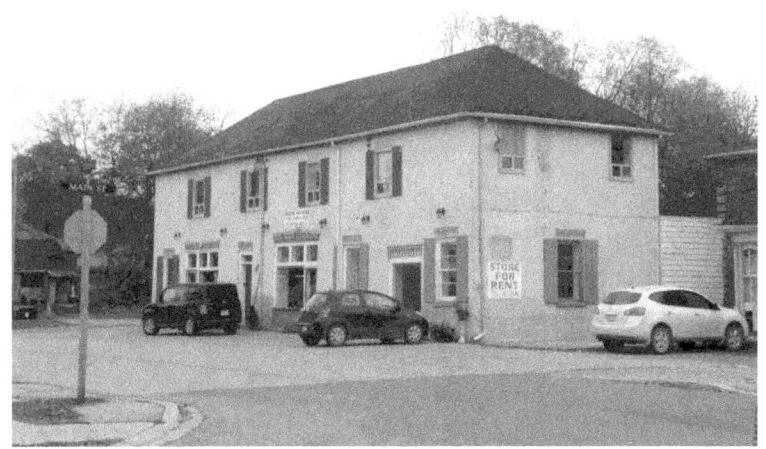

Corner of Main Street

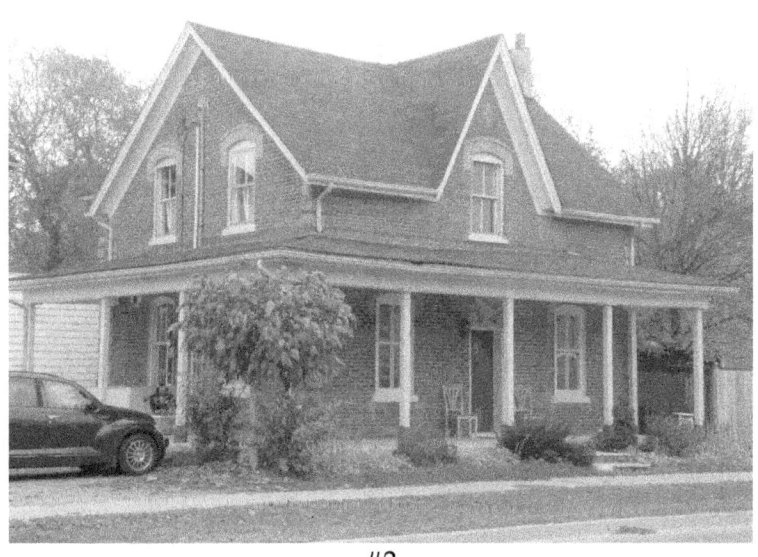

#3

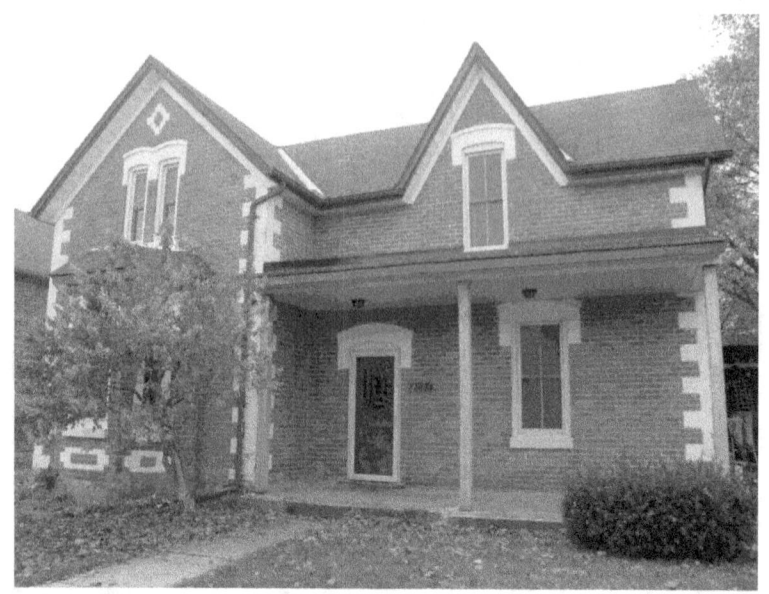

#180

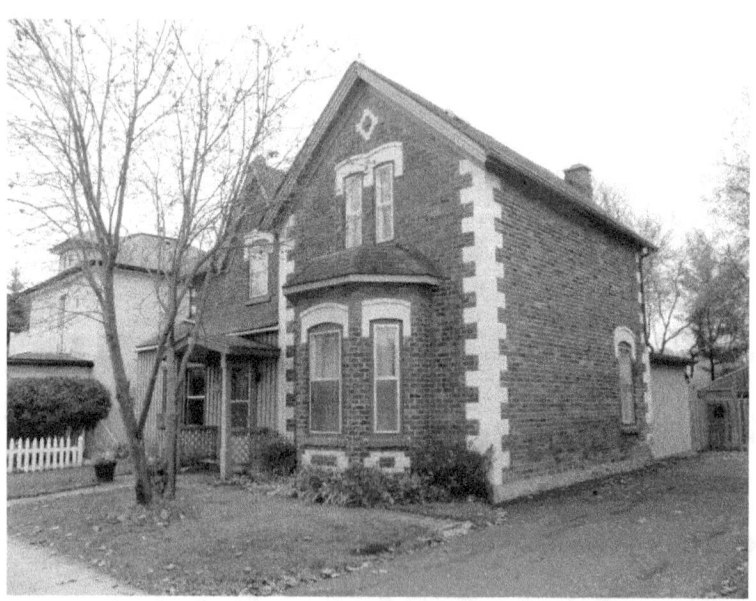

#178

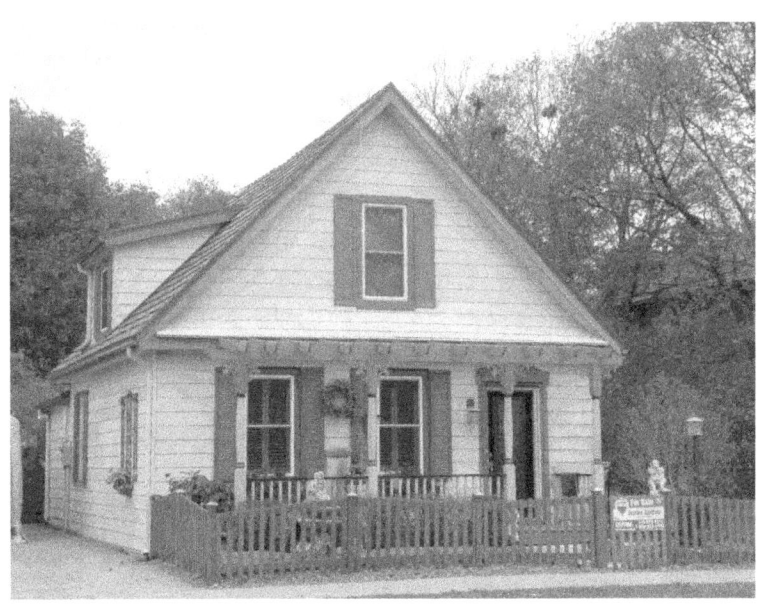

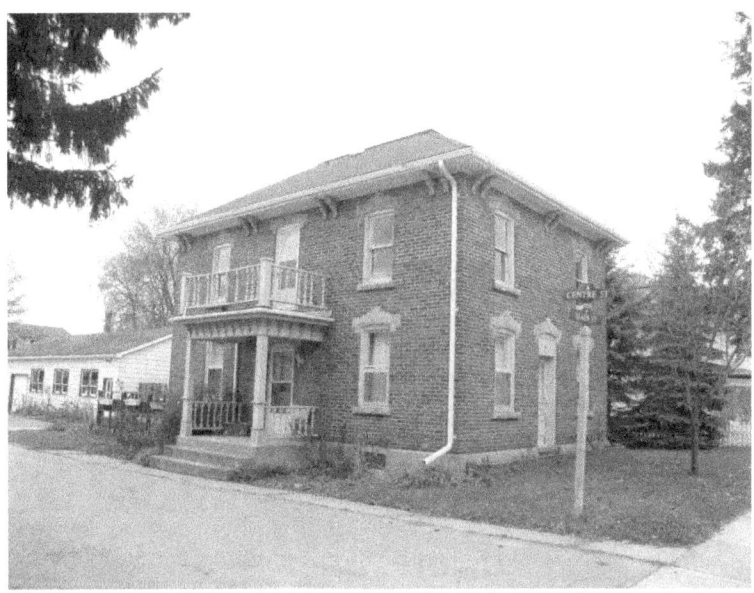

Corner of Centre and Main Streets
paired cornice brackets

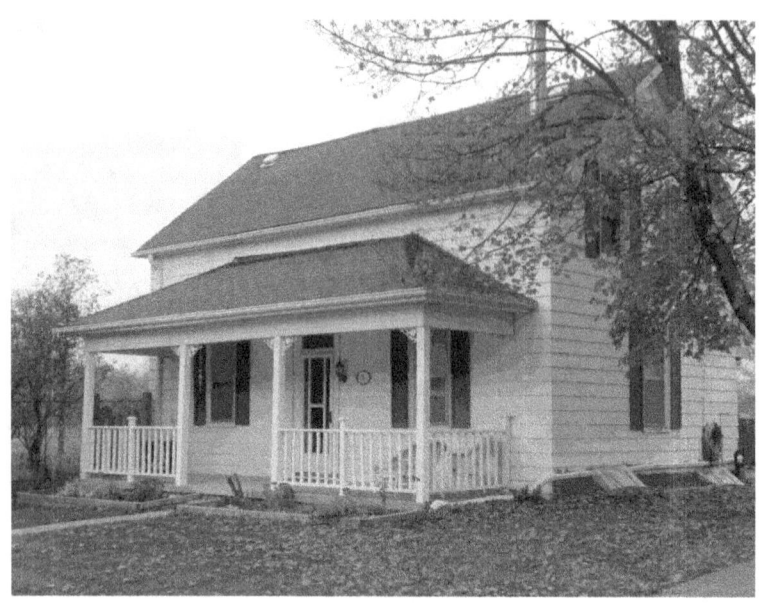

#3

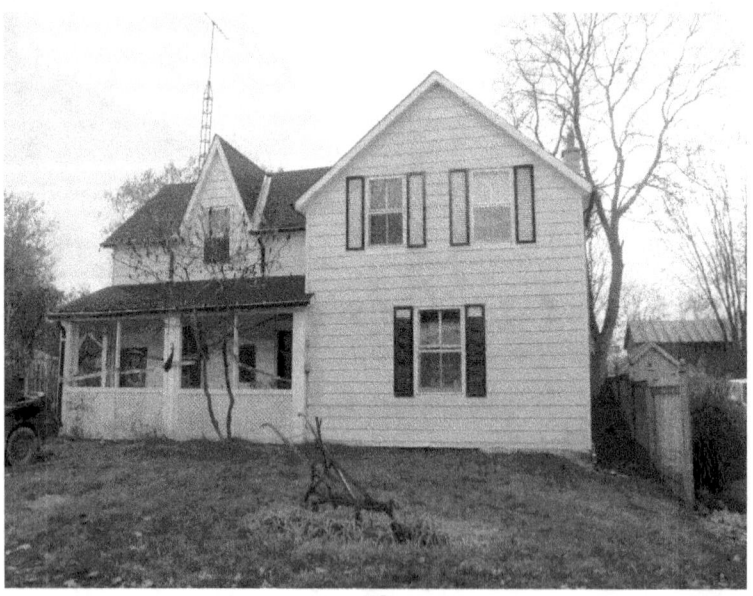

#2

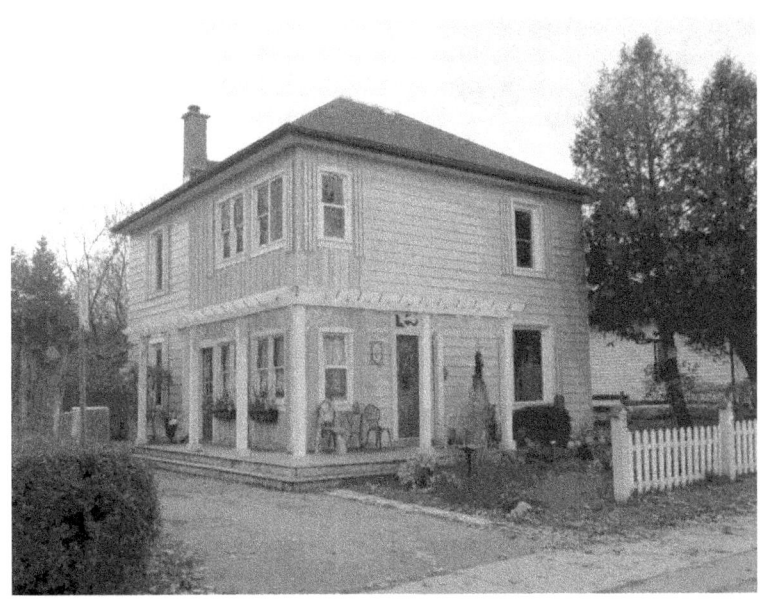

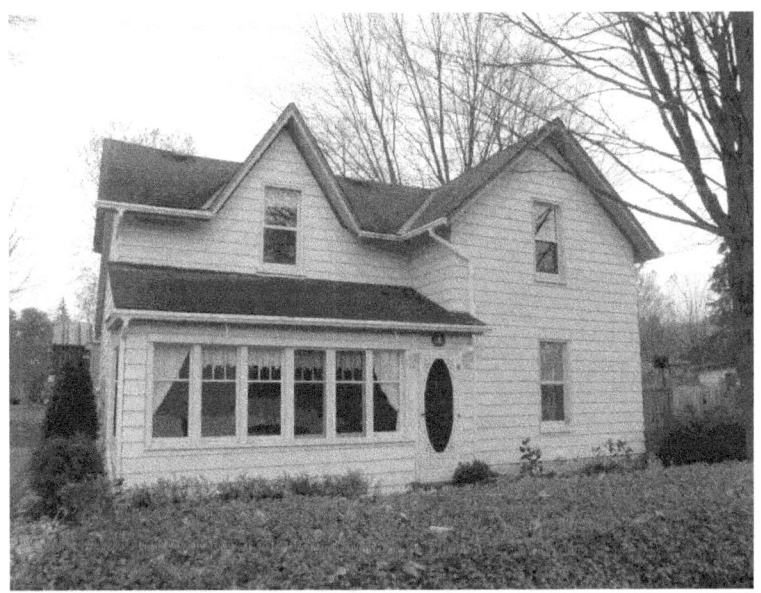

4 Centre Street

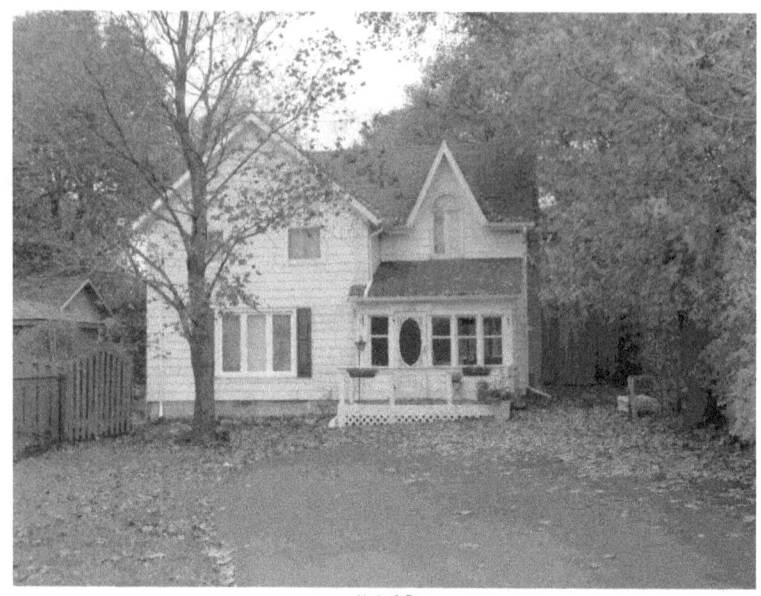

#169

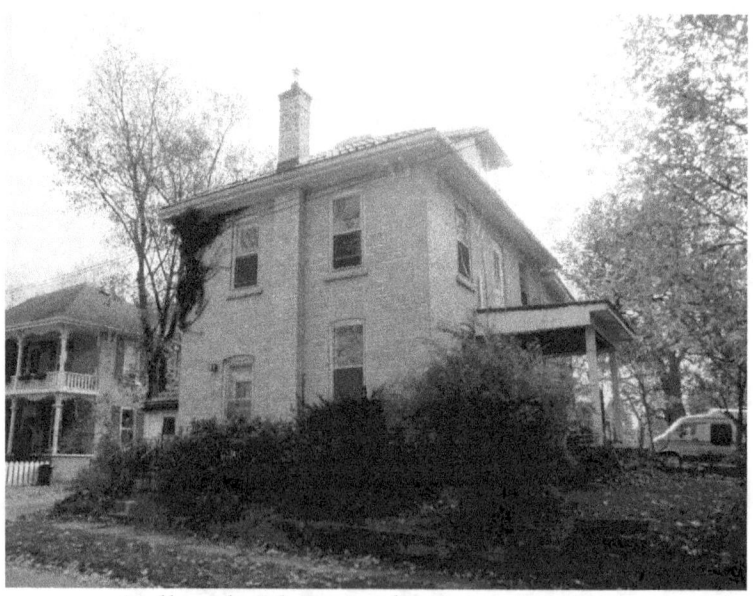

Yellow brick, paired cornice brackets

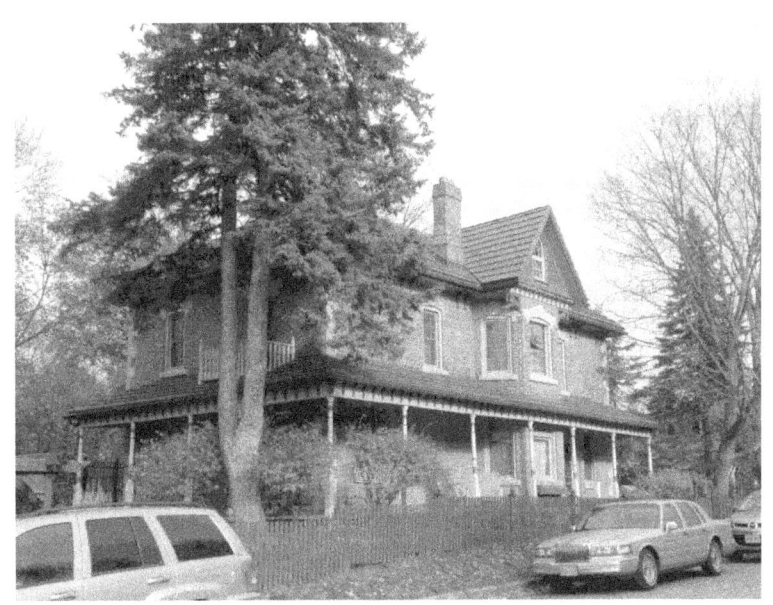

#2

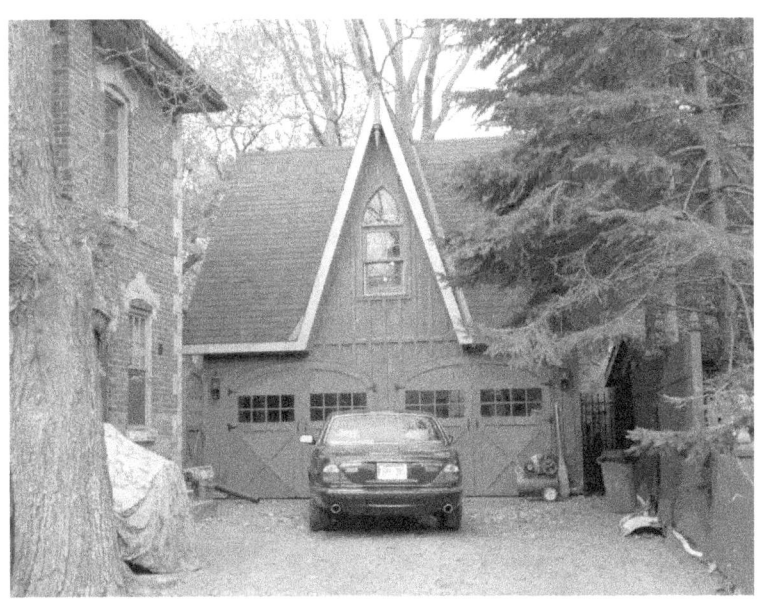

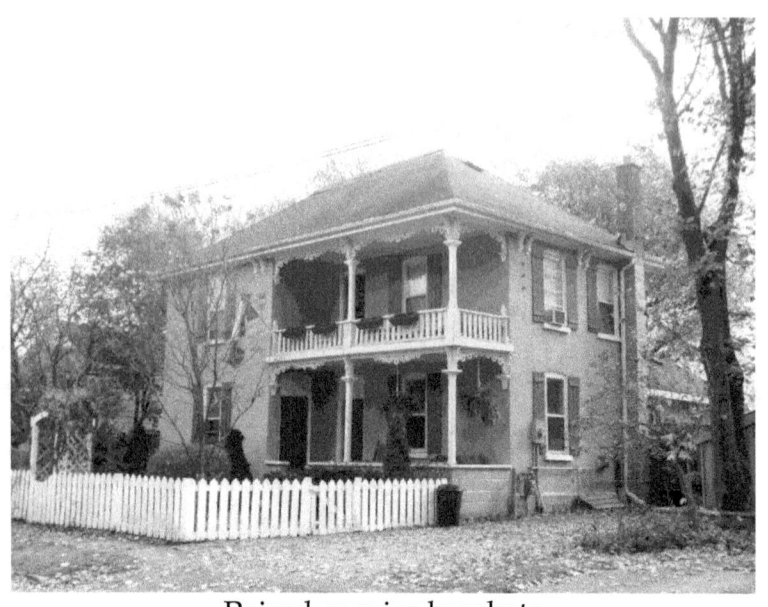

Paired cornice brackets

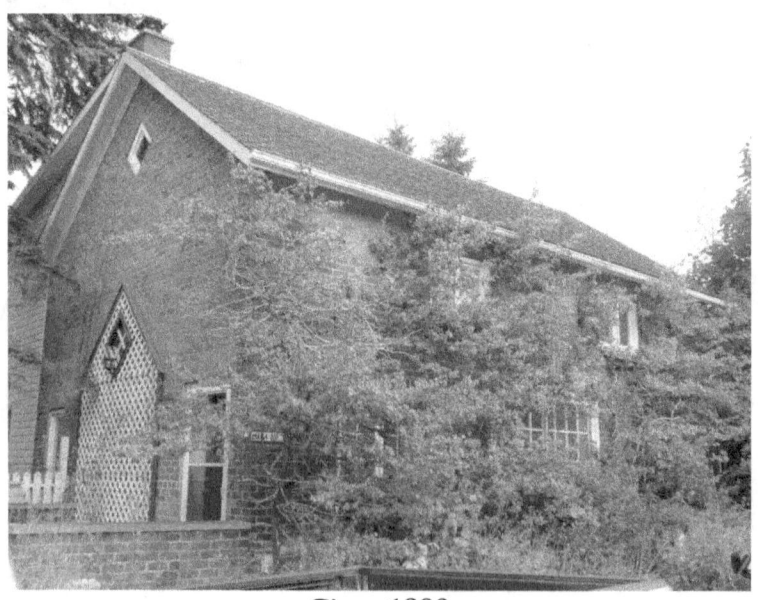

Circa 1890

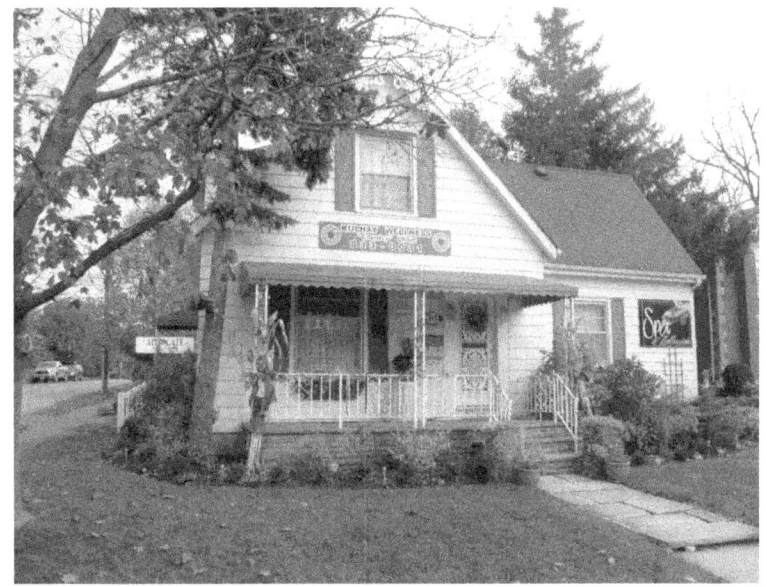

#165

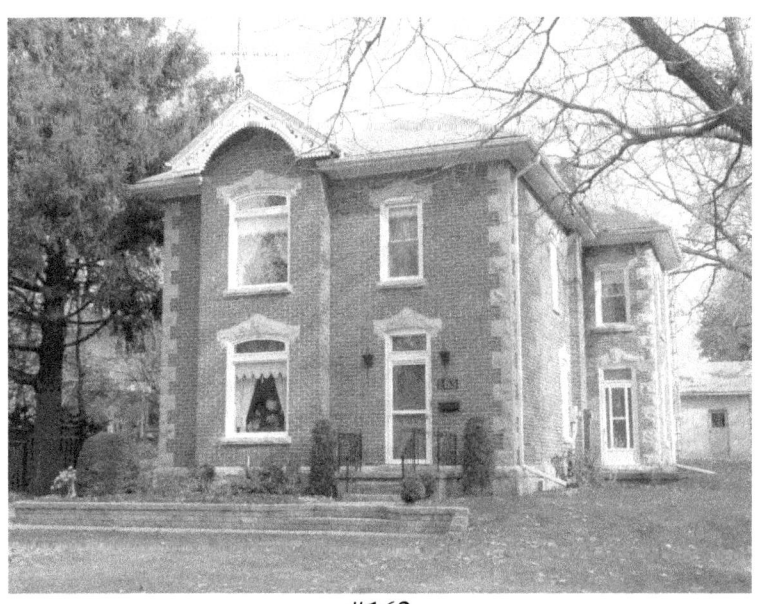

#163

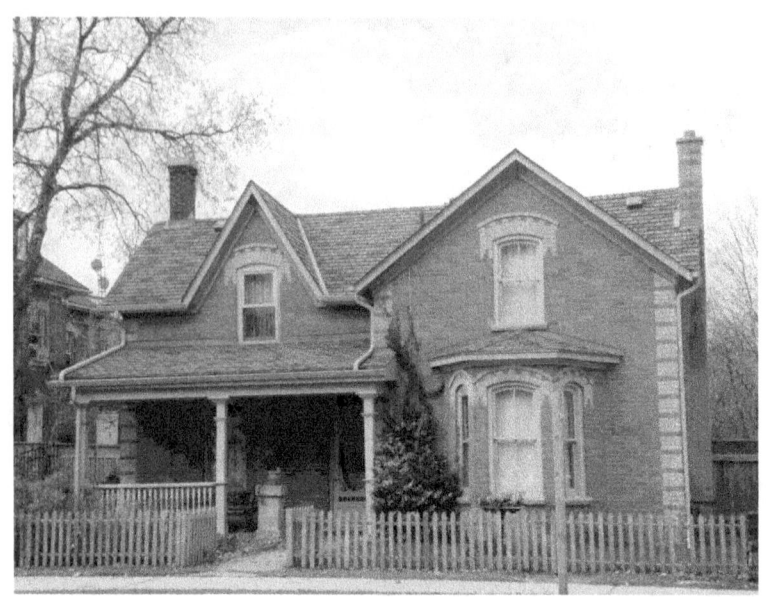

#158

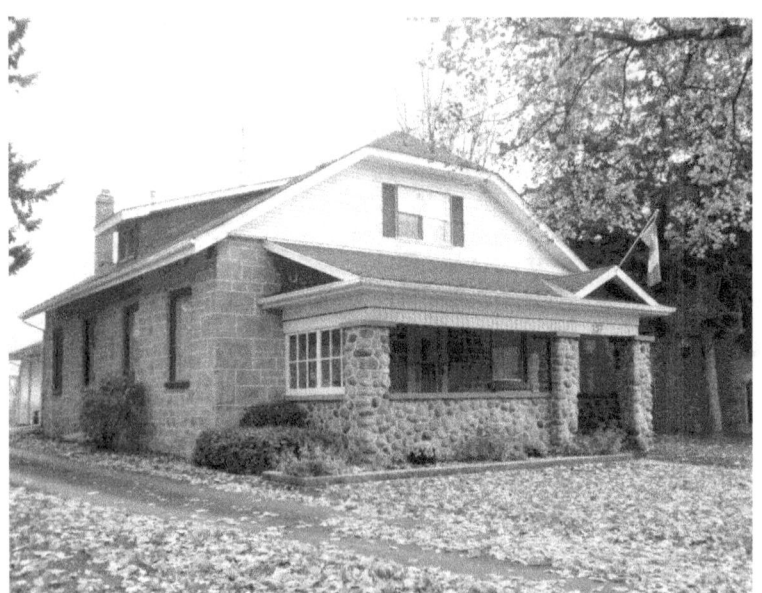

#157

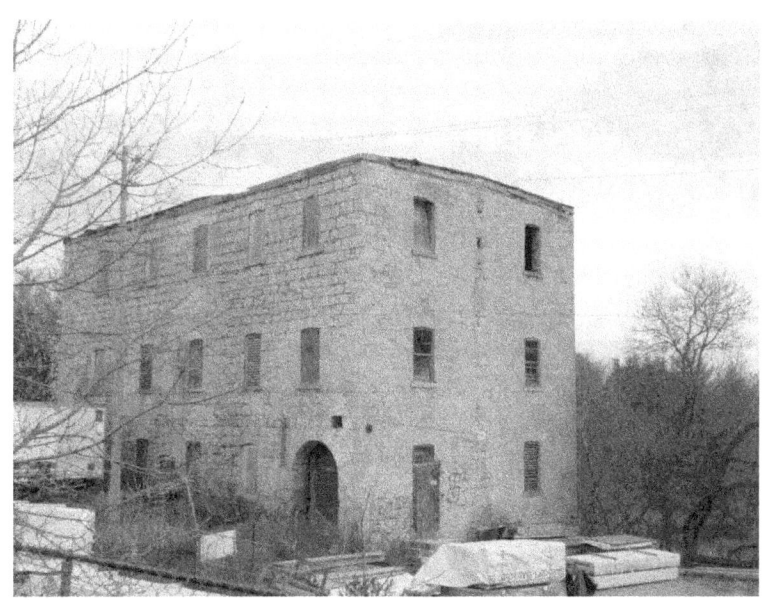

Old mill

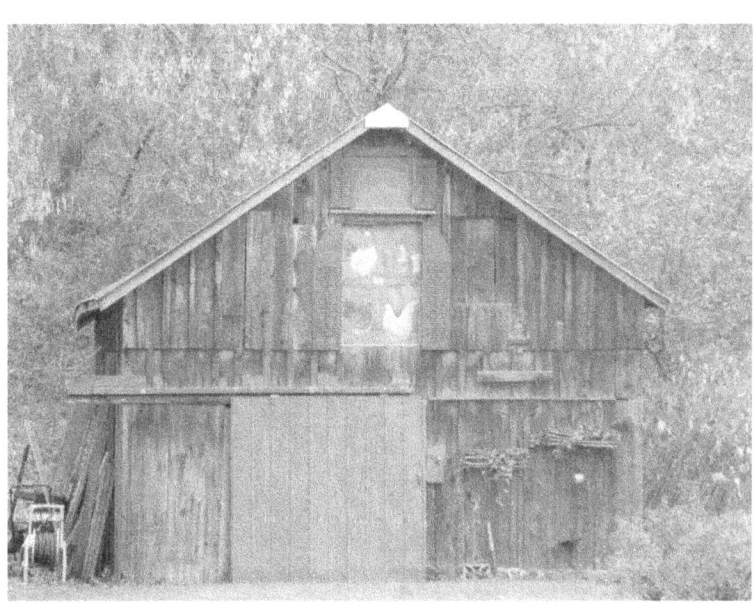

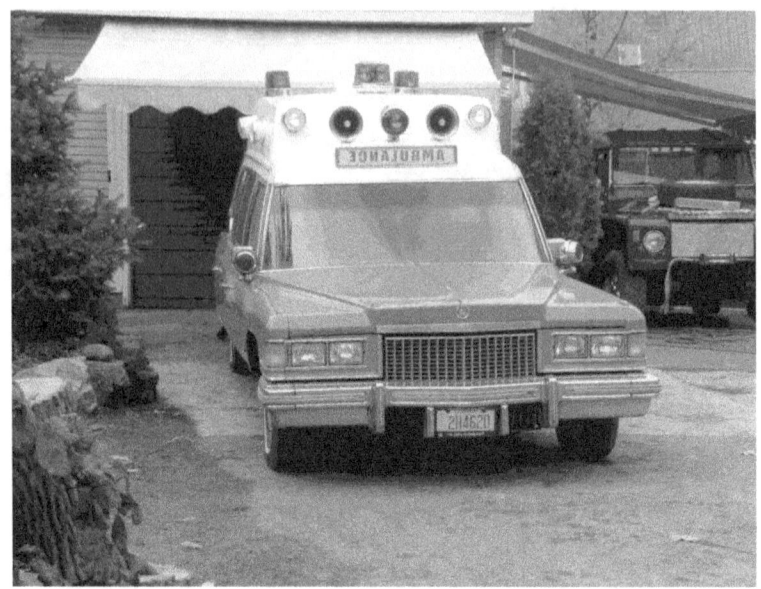

Old ambulance

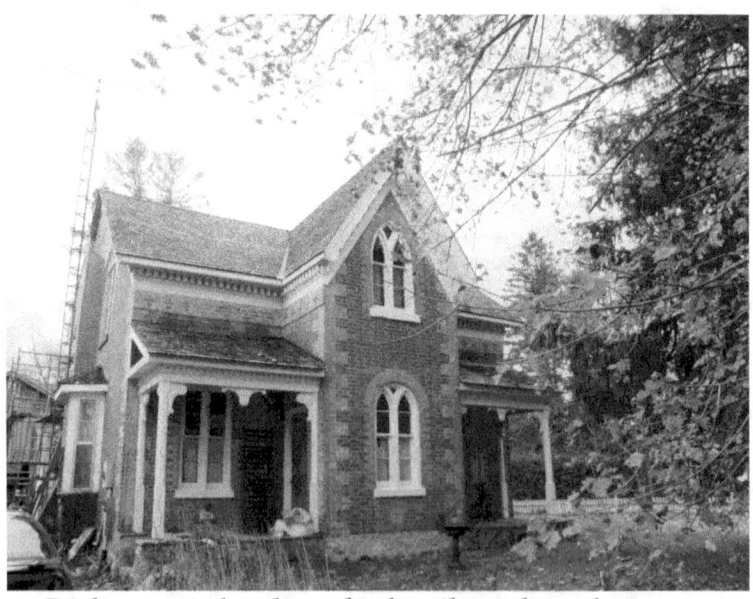

Dichromatic brickwork, dentil work under eaves

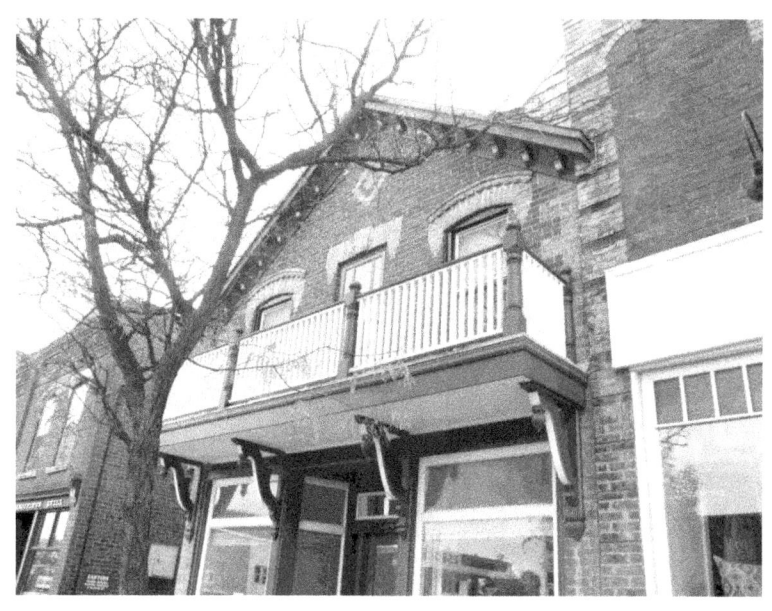

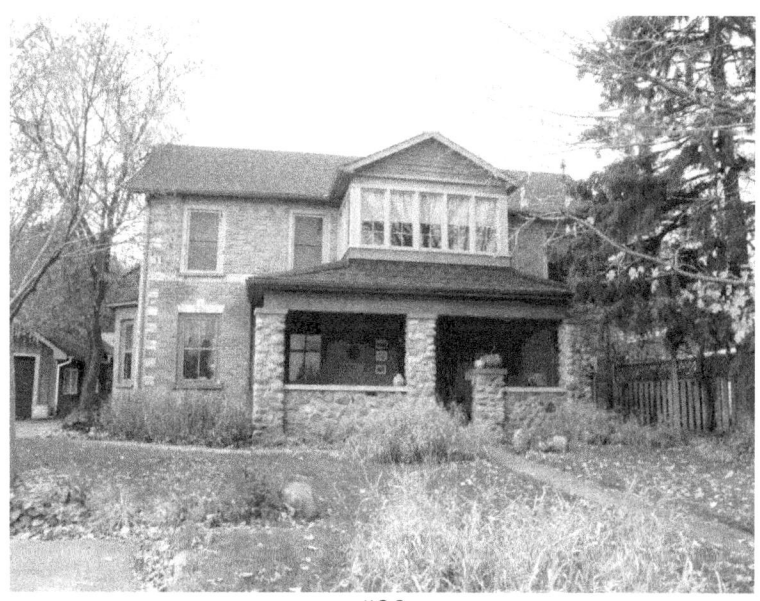

#30